WORKING IN CANVAS

WORKING IN CANVAS

BY

P. W BLANDFORD

Associate of the Royal Institution of Naval Architecture

Author of "Netmaking," etc.

GLASGOW

BROWN, SON & FERGUSON, LIMITED

52 DARNLEY STREET

First Edition - - 1965
Second Edition - 1981

ISBN 0 85174 416 8

Printed and Made in Great Britain

PREFACE

CANVAS has a great many uses, both ashore and afloat. Although it may be felt to have reached its peak of usefulness in the heyday of sailing ships, it is now used for a greater variety of purposes, by professional and amateur seamen, and by those who seek their livelihood and recreation ashore. The development of synthetic fibres has stimulated interest.

Although sails are rarely found on commercial craft, the man who goes to sea professionally still uses canvas for covers, screens, awnings and similar things. Someone on board needs to know how to make and service these things. Yachtsmen know that sails are used more than ever before. Although most yachtsmen would hesitate to make their own sails, they should be able to carry out repairs and alterations. Ashore, the camper is a considerable user of canvas. He can repair tents and make new equipment. Canvas covers are used in many trades. Canvas bags and cases are used for many purposes.

The author does not know of another complete book on canvas working. Many seamanship books touch on it. Even books on sails do not offer much instruction on the practical details of hand work. This book is an attempt to bring together all the basic information on making things from canvas, in the hope that it will be of value to everyone concerned with using this material.

P. W. BLANDFORD.

CONTENTS

BIBLIOGRAPHY

Books on related subjects

The Boatswain's Manual, by Wm. McLeod

Knots and Splices, by Jutsum

Netmaking, by P. W. Blandford

Rope Splicing, by P. W. Blandford

(All above published by Brown, Son & Ferguson, Ltd.)

Sails, by Jeremy Howard-Williams (Granada)

The Care and Repair of Sails, by Jeremy Howard-Williams (Granada)

Modern Sailmaking, by P. W. Blandford (Tab Books, U.S.A.)

WORKING IN CANVAS

CHAPTER I.

TOOLS AND MATERIALS

CANVASWORK involves sewing, of a rather special sort. In most cases the materials are comparatively heavy and the equipment used has to be of a robust type accordingly. Machine sewing has to be done on substantial machines, basically similar to the domestic sewing machine. Hand sewing has to allow for the considerable force often needed to make a stitch. Consequently, although canvaswork has much in common with domestic needlework, the work is altogether heavier and tougher.

Almost all hand sewing is done with sail needles. These have a triangular section through the blade, with a short narrower round section between the blade and the eye (Fig. 1*a*). The triangular part forces a hole large enough to give a good clearance to the thread, doubled through the eye. Needles are normally made of cast steel and are supplied highly polished. They are not rustproof and care should be taken to prevent rust, as this makes sewing difficult. A tubular case (Fig. 1*b*) may be used. The needles may be pushed into a cork, which is then pushed into a

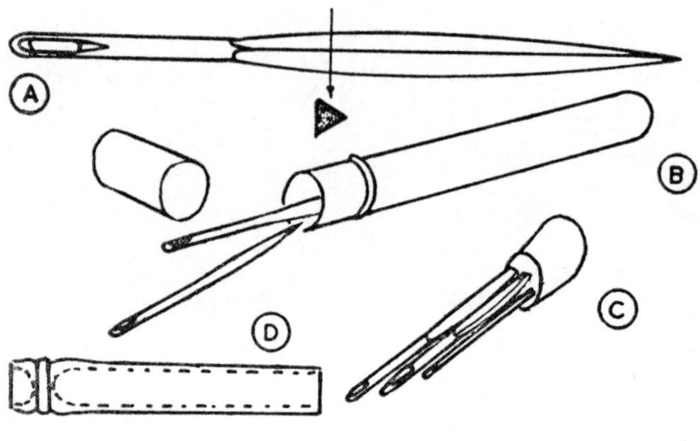

FIG. 1

tube (Fig. 1*c*). A section of bamboo may be made into a case (Fig 1*d*). Needles may be wrapped in a piece of oiled cloth.

Needles are made in sizes, graded by a number which corresponds to the thickness of the round part measured by the Standard Wire Gauge. Sizes range from No. 4, which is 6 in. long by 4 gauge (0·23 in.), to No. 18, which is $2\frac{1}{8}$ in. long by 18 gauge (0·048 in.). The table (Fig. 2) gives the range of sizes made, although in practice only sizes 9 to 18 are in common use. For yacht sails, canvas covers and awnings, or similar work, most needs are taken care of by sizes 13 to 16.

There are a great many other types of needles, favoured by particular trades. Nearly all of a canvasworker's needs are taken care of by the common sailmaker's needles, but he should know about some of the othe types. Packing, or

SAIL NEEDLE SIZES

No.	Length inches	Gauge S.W.G.	Thick-ness inches	Suggested use
4	6	4	0·232	Extra large
5	5½	5	0·212	Double hand line
6	5	6	0·192	Large hand line
7	4¾	7	0·176	Middle hand line
8	4½	8	0·160	Small hand line
9	4	9	0·144	Large marline
10	3¾	10	0·128	Small marline
11	3½	11	0·116	Double bolt rope
12	3¼	12	0·104	Large bolt rope
13	3	13	0·092	Small bolt rope
14	2¾	14	0·080	Large seaming
14½	2⅝	14½	0·076	Middle seaming
15	2½	15	0·072	Small seaming
16	2⅜	16	0·064	Tabling
17	2¼	17	0·056	Flat seam
18	2⅛	18	0·048	Extra small

bagging, needles are used for sewing hessian and other coarse fabrics (Fig. 3*a*). They are longer

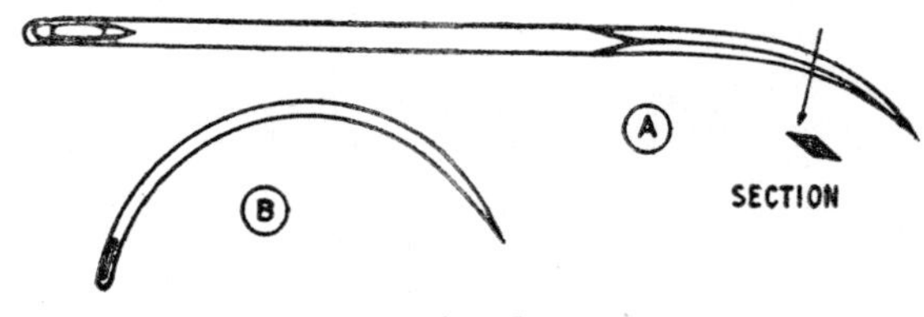

Fig. 3

and thinner, and the blades have diamond sections. Curved needles are used in several trades (Fig. 3*b*). The leatherworker favours an oval section and a triangular point. A curved mattress needle may be round all the way. The upholsterer has his needles pointed at both ends. Curved needles are useful in canvas repair work, where the job can only be tackled from one side. Upholsterers also use some very long straight needles. Needlemakers also produce a variety of pins, spikes and prickers; some of which have their uses in canvaswork. Most of the needles used in the world are made in Redditch, Worcestershire, England.

Sail needles are pushed through the canvas with a palm (Fig. 4*a*). Although it may be possible to push a needle through thin fabric without one, or to push through stouter material by bearing down on a bench, a palm is the accepted tool and a canvasworker should have and use at least one palm. The basic palm is designed to wear on the right hand. It is made of leather, with a hole for the thumb and an iron plate set below it for pushing the needle. Some means of adjusting for size is provided. Lefthanded palms are also made, but their use is unusual, even by lefthanded people.

Palms are made of stout leather, which may be stiffened by treatment. The makers call the strongest ones *Sailmakers'* palms and the lighter ones *Sailors'* palms. There are many varieties, but the broad division is between the seaming

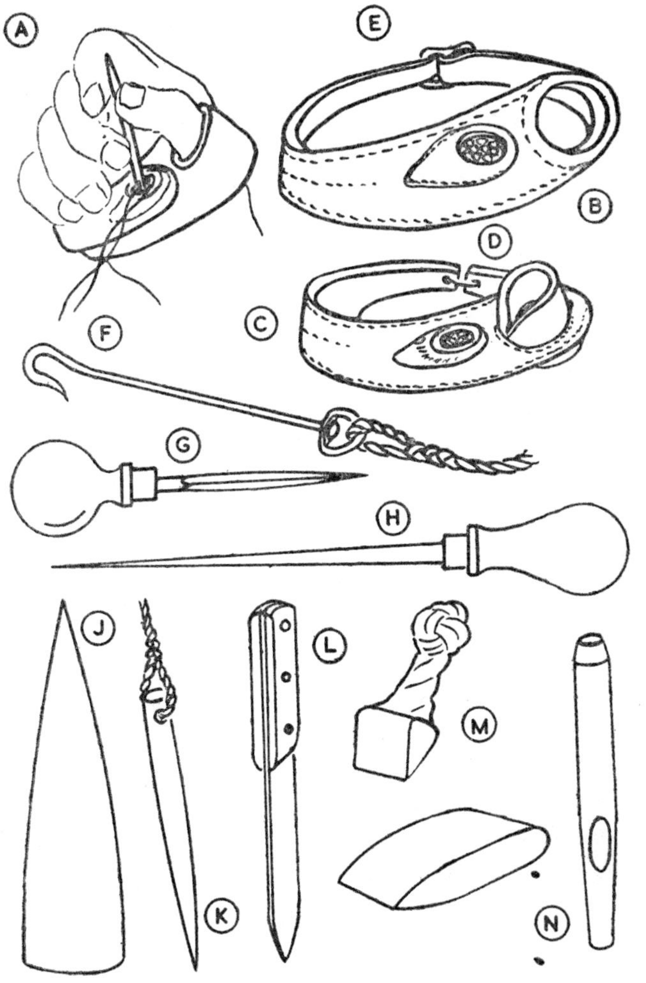

FIG. 4.

palm (Fig. 4*b*) and the roping palm (Fig. 4*c*), which has extra stiffening and protection around the thumb. For a palm to be used by an individual worker, the expert favours an adjustment made by tying the ends behind the hand with thread (Fig. 4*d*), but if a palm is likely to be used by several people, it is more convenient to have a buckle (Fig. 4*e*). The iron block has a pattern of hollows in it to take the needle end, and it should be set well into the leather to reduce the risk of slipping out.

A sailmaker uses a stool or form, with his tools pushed into holes at one end. This is a low backless bench, on which he sits with the work across his knees. The occasional canvas worker may not need a special bench, but the most convenient way to tackle most jobs is to sit low, wearing a stout canvas apron to protect the clothes and guard the legs from pricks with the needle.

When sewing a seam it is a help to have a sail hook (Fig. 4*f*). This may have a plain eye, although it is better if there is a swivel. A light lanyard is attached to the eye. The hook goes into the end of the seam, the lanyard is attached somewhere firm, and one hand keeps a tension on the canvas while sewing is done with the other hand. Without a hook there may be a tendency for the parts to move in relation to each other so that the seam finishes with more tension on one piece than the other.

One or two spikes are useful. A small spike

with a triangular point, like a needle, will make holes and open them out (Fig. 4*g*). A rather stouter round spike has its uses (Fig. 4*h*). These may be sold as ice picks. For pushing grommets into shape and similar jobs, a fid is worth having. This is a hardwood spike, obtainable in many sizes (Fig. 4*j*). A large one will do all that a small one will if it tapers evenly to a point. A steel marline spike (Fig. 4*k*) will deal with smaller jobs. Both tools are also used if ropes have to be spliced to the canvas.

Although light canvas may be cut with scissors, the canvasworker does most of his cutting with a knife. The most useful one has a thin blade and a handle made by riveting wood each side of the steel (Fig. 4*l*). An oilstone and oilcan are needed to keep the knife sharp. The points of needles and spikes may also need occasional touching up.

The back of the knife blade should be rounded, so that it can be used for rubbing down folds in the canvas. For heavier seams there may be a special seam rubber. Traditionally this might be elaborately carved in hard wood or bone, but a plain piece of hardwood will do (Fig. 4*m*). A hard plastic could be used.

Many holes are made by pushing a spike through, but sometimes a circle of canvas has to be removed. This is done with a hollow punch (Fig. 4*n*), used with a hammer over a wood block. For light canvas there are plier-type punches, in which the hollow punch on one side closes against a brass anvil on the other side. For fixing eyelets and press studs there are special punches, and these are described in Chapter 4.

Materials:

The word *canvas* is a general term covering many materials and with different shades of meaning in different countries. It may be assumed to mean rather heavier grades of cloth than would be used for clothing and similar purposes, but even then there are some very light grades of modern materials used in sail-making that might warrant the description of canvas. For centuries canvas was only made from natural materials, but at the end of World War II there came a revolution, with synthetic fabrics almost completely taking over from those made from natural fibres. Natural fibre canvases are still in use, but most of the canvas in use today is made from man-made fibres.

Of the natural materials, in the past most British canvas was made of flax, while most American canvas was cotton. Hemp was also used, and it is a corruption of its Latin name which produced the name 'canvas'. Jute and tow were also used. Jute is still met in the coarse-weave sacking material, called hessian in Britain and burlap in America.

There are a great many synthetic materials used to make modern canvas. Some of these can be made with different characteristics, and there are new materials and variations being produced, so it is sometimes difficult to keep pace with canvases and cloths available or to recognise them. However, there are a few established synthetics that are most commonly used. One of the oldest is *nylon*, which is a polyamide fibre plastic derived from coal. It is more elastic than most natural materials and other synthetics, so it is unsuitable where the article being made has to keep its shape and size. In sailmaking its particular use is in spinnakers. Polyester fabric is the other well-known synthetic fabric, usually known by its trade names of *Terylene* and *Dacron*.

In natural canvases the threads are made up of a large number of comparatively short pieces, giving a slight hairy feel. In synthetic cloths the threads are made up of continuous lengths, which are better called filaments. As there are no breaks, except accidental ones, the finished cloth is much smoother. Similar materials are used for ropes, and where the hairiness is wanted to provide grip, some synthetic ropes are treated to give that feel on the exterior, but this is not done with canvas.

Canvas is manufactured on a loom. The threads running lengthwise are called the *warp*. Those crossing the cloth are the *weft*. The weft threads turn back at each edge of the cloth, leaving a firm line there without loose ends. This manufactured edge is called the *selvedge*. At one time all canvas had a coloured thread woven in parallel with each selvedge, but now these *selvedge stripes* are less common. Their purpose was to act as guides to overlap when making seams.

When canvas was only made from natural materials it was sometimes graded by number, but this system is rarely used now. There were seven grades, going from No. 0, which was very stout, to No. 6, which was lightest and softest. Some words never had precise meanings. *Duck* was assumed to be good quality cotton canvas. *Tarpaulin* was a rough, heavy grade, but the name is now used for any covering sheet. *Sail cloth* now means any of the lighter canvases used for sails, but it used to be meant to indicate a good quality light cotton canvas.

Canvas is made in many widths, both Imperial and metric measure. It is graded by weight. The logical way is by area, but in America it may be by linear yard with a width of 28½ inches. In Britain the quoted weight is per square yard, although some canvas is graded in a similar way metrically. If British and American methods of grading are to be compared, the proportion 4:5 gives a close approximation, as an American 4-oz. canvas would be the same as a British 5-oz. one.

Natural fibre canvases for such things as tents, boat covers and awnings are usually between 8-oz. and 15-oz. grades. Synthetic fibre fabrics are stronger, so their weights may be rather less. For small boat sails the grades may be under 4 oz., and they are broken down into decimal divisions. One area where natural fibre fabrics are still usual is in tent making. Natural fibre fabric will allow the moisture produced by sleeping people to escape while still keeping rain out, but synthetic fabrics that keep out rain also keep moisture in and cause condensation.

The natural fabrics will absorb moisture and may rot if left wet without any protective treatment. Of the synthetic materials, only nylon will absorb moisture and that is slight compared with natural fibres. For most uses, natural fibre canvases are proofed. While keeping out water, this also gives some resistance to rot. The proofing solution may also be used to colour the canvas. Proofing is best done during manufacture, but proofing solutions can be bought to apply by brushing, spraying and soaking. Some solutions will also give fire-retardent properties. The effect of proofing does not last long, and periodic reproofing is advisable. There are special proofing applicators for dealing with sewn seams, as these may need attention more often than the body of the canvas.

There are several canvases coated with plastic—usually P.V.C.—on one or both sides. This gives a smooth waterproof surface, although it is possible to provide a texture—a common example being imitation leather. The smooth grades are used for covers, canoe skins, tent groundsheets and similar things. The strength is in the canvas and not the coating, so this should be chosen accordingly.

The thread used should suit the material and

grade of the canvas. For natural fabrics the thread for hand sewing is called *seaming twine* or *sail twine*. It is more like fine string than domestic sewing thread. Terylene and other synthetic materials are also used for making sail twine. They should be used for synthetic canvases, but they may also be preferable for some natural fibre canvases. In use, it is often the stitching that fails before the canvas, so the greater strength and resistance to rot of synthetic twine may be an advantage. However, it will not stretch a comparable amount to some natural fibre canvases, and that may be a disadvantage.

Natural fibre threads are usually waxed before use. This rubs down the loose hairs, strengthens the thread and gives it some degree of waterproofness. The thread may be bought waxed, but even then, most workers will pull the thread through a ball of beeswax or a piece of candle before sewing. Synthetic threads do not require waxing to waterproof them and there are few hairs to stick down, but waxing helps to make stitches stay put as they are made, so it is usual to wax all thread.

Some sail twine is sold in hanks, but care is needed to avoid tangles when drawing out a length. Larger quantities are on cops, which are tubular card reels. Synthetic sail twine is better on a plastic reel. Reels to suit machine work are supplied to fit particular sewing machines.

If natural fibre fabrics are heated they will char and then burn. If synthetic fibre fabrics are heated they will melt. Heat from the sun will not cause melting, nor will a moderate amount of friction, but if heat is deliberately applied, the material can be melted to seal it. With synthetic rope, the ends may be heated with a flame and rolled to consolidate them while still semi-molten, to prevent fraying and reduce the need for whipping.

One way of sealing a cut edge of synthetic cloth is to run a hot soldering bit along it, so the ends of the threads melt and bond together. If a narrow soldering bit is available it can be used like a knife to cut and seal edges in one operation. However, the sealed edge tends to be hard, and the technique is unsuitable for all situations. Any cloth, whether natural or synthetic material, may be cut with a zig-zag edge, using pinking shears, and it will then resist fraying.

CHAPTER II

BASIC SEWING

Machine sewing is quicker and neater than hand sewing, but it is only practicable for the lighter canvases and for longer seams. Much canvaswork has to be done by hand, and there is a satisfaction and fascination about producing a neat piece of hand sewing, once the basic techniques have been mastered.

Some of the lighter synthetic materials can be sewn on a domestic sewing machine, but the heavier canvases need special equipment. Although electric power is desirable, much sewing has to be done away from a power source, so hand machines for canvaswork are commoner now than their domestic counterparts.

Zig-zag stitching is desirable. It looks better than straight stitching and allows for slight stretch, so it is easier to get joined cloths even. Straight stitching is needed on some parts of a sail and on other canvaswork. Learn the adjustments on the machine and do some experimental stitching before tackling serious work. Learn about *tension*, to get the knot in the middle of the thickness of cloth and *stitch length* to get a correct stitch form and size.

Most of the descriptions in this book apply to hand sewing. Adaption to machine sewing will be obvious. Where hand stitches are made over a folded edge, machine stitching can be made close to and parallel with the edge. It is possible to use zig-zag stitching over a cut edge, so the stitches prevent fraying. Only half the width of the stitching is holding the edge, so this is only suitable for light loading. For strength it would be better to turn under the edge and sew on top, close to the edge.

Some things, like roping a sail edge in the traditional way, can only be done by hand sewing, but there are some modern alternatives that permit machine sewing. The rope may be enclosed in a sewn tube, either a separate piece which is then sewn to the sail or the tabled edge of the sail can enclose the rope. An alternative is to substitute tape for the rope and sew on the cloth. In some sails the rope edge has to be wire, and that can only be held in a canvas tube.

Control of a needle and dexterity in its use needs practice. At first the palm may feel clumsy and the work may progress very slowly, but after a little experience the quality and speed of the work should improve considerably.

The amount of thread or twine used each time depends to a certain extent on personal preference. For most purposes the thread is used double. If a considerable length has to be pulled through after each stitch, progress will be slow, although joins will be infrequent. A short length allows much quicker work, but joins will occur more often. A reasonable length for a new piece of doubled thread allows the arm to almost fully extend after making a stitch.

For most hand work the stitches should be about five per inch. A wider spacing looks untidy and gives the impression of haste. A slightly closer spacing may be possible, but in average canvas, using sail twine, stitches closer than six per inch are not practicable.

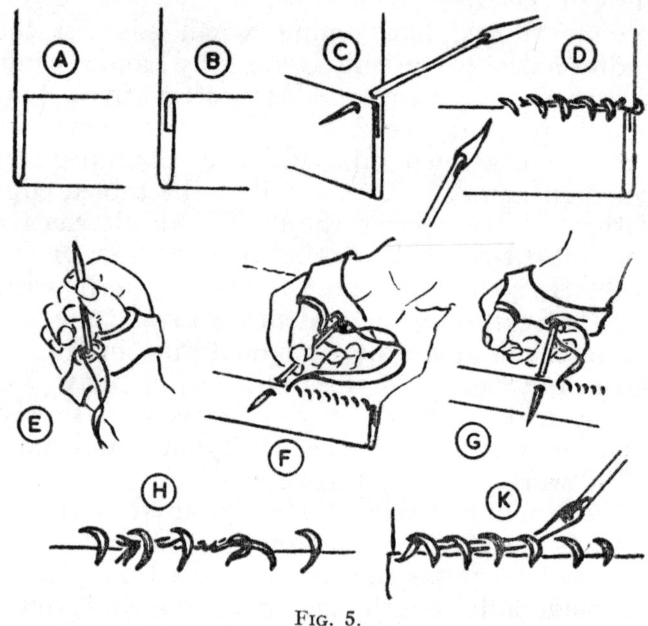

Fig. 5.

Most stitching is a simple over-and-over action. Most right-handed workers will find that the most convenient way to do this is to work from right to left, stitching in a way that points the needle towards the body when it enters the canvas.

Tabling makes a good job for practice. Most edges have to be turned in. This may be to strengthen them, or to provide a tube for a draw string. If it is a selvedge, the edge can be merely turned down (Fig. 5*a*). If it is a cut edge, the raw edge should be turned under so that it will not fray (Fig. 5*b*). Make the folds by hand then rub them down on a smooth surface, either with the back of a knife or a wooden rubber. The width of the tabling depends on its purpose, but for the neck of a kit bag in 12 oz. canvas it could be about 1 in.

With the tabling uppermost and pointing away from the body, rest the canvas across the knees. Enter the needle through the body of the canvas near the end (Fig. 5*c*). Let the point come up through the edge of the tabling. Pull through, until the ends are within about 1 in. of the hole. Lay these ends along the seam and continue to sew over them (Fig. 5*d*). If the ends are covered by three or four tight stitches the joint should be secure.

Continue stitching. Aim to enter close to the turned in edge and come out at the same distance from it each time, while keep ng the stitches at regular intervals. Maintain a tension that will make a secure joint without pulling the canvas into a crease. With the left hand maintain the tabling parallel. A few pencil marks may be advisable, if there is no selvedge stripe to act as a guide. If the seam is long, put a hook through the righthand end after a few inches have been done and fasten its lanyard somewhere to your right. Pull against this with your left hand while stitching.

The use of the palm will be discovered. Hold the needle between the first finger and thumb with the eye end resting on the iron pad (Fig. 5*e*). As the needle point is inserted in the canvas thrust with the palm (Fig. 5*f*). Once it has entered, greater pressure can be applied by releasing the needle and concentrating on the push (Fig. 5*g*). As the point emerges, grip it again and guide it out, ready to pull through the thread and start the next stitch. A stage will be reached where the whole process is almost one continuous action. The smallest needles may be too short for the point to be held comfortably while the eye end is on the iron pad, but the sizes used with average weight canvas allow holding and pushing comfortably.

If a new piece of thread has to be joined in, cut off the needle to leave at least an inch of the ends. Thread the needle with a new piece and make a stitch alongside the last one. Pull through all but an inch, then lay the old and new ends along the seam, preferably twisted together (Fig. 5*h*). Continue to sew over these ends so that they are gripped by about four stitches.

When the end of the seam is reached make the last four stitches loosely then pass the needle back under them (Fig. 5*k*), Tighten each stitch in turn, either with the point of the needle or a spike. Pull the thread through and cut off, to leave the end similar in appearance to the start of the seam.

When edges have to be joined, either to make up the width or to complete a construction, such as a cylindrical bag, the best joint is a flat seam (Fig. 6). The two edges are overlapped. If they are selvedges they need not be turned in (Fig. 6*a*), but if they have been cut, they should be turned under and rubbed down (Fig. 6*b*). There may, of course, be one selvedge and one cut edge. Only the latter need be turned under, although both could be for the sake of a balanced appearance. The amount of overlap depends on circumstances, but between ¾ in. and 1½ in. should suit most jobs.

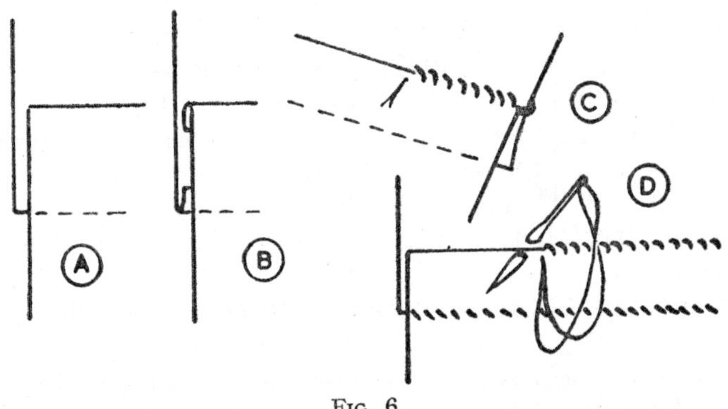

Fig. 6.

Treat the first edge in the same way as when tabling, although if the end is to be unsupported by another part, it is worth while taking one or two turns over the end before starting to stitch along the seam (Fig. 6*c*). Mark the amount of overlap at intervals on the lower piece so as to maintain an even width. On a long seam it may be an advantage to put in a few temporary large tacking stitches at intervals to hold the parts in the correct relation to each other.

When sewing the first edge of a flat seam there is a tendency for the lower cloth to shorten slightly. As the stitches are made it creeps in a little. If it is possible to leave trimming to length until after the line of stitches is made, this can be put right, otherwise it is better to start with the lower cloth a little too long.

After sewing one edge of a flat seam, turn the whole job over so as to bring the new edge pointing away from you, then sew again from the right (Fig. 6*d*). A sail hook should be used, and the left hand should keep a good tension on the job. Watch that both pieces are kept flat in relation to each other. Careless work can cause one piece to pucker in relation to the other.

When both edges of the flat seam have been sewn, stretch the seam and pull the body of the cloth so as to get the lines of stitches flat. If necessary, lightly hammer them to get the thread flat.

A flat seam is very strong, due to the two lines of stitches. Sometimes a single line of stitching may be considered strong enough. For this purpose a round seam is used (Fig. 7). The method leaves raw edges on one side, but for many purposes this does not matter.

The two edges which are to meet should be folded back towards the side which will be inside or the least important (Fig. 7*a*). The amount folded need not be very much—½ in. will do for most canvas. The sides which will be outside are brought together (Fig. 7*b*).

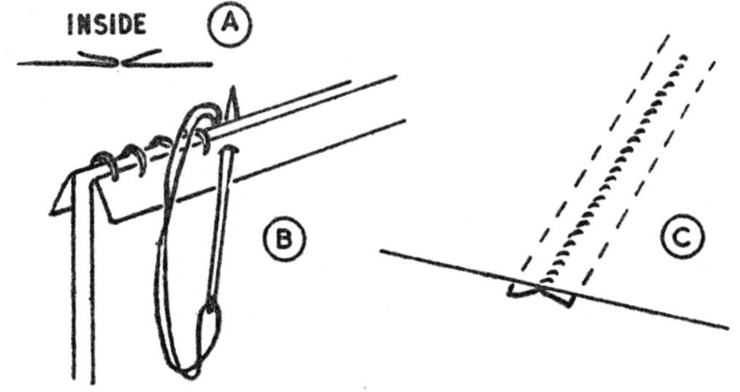

Fig. 7.

This seam is more conveniently sewn with the canvas held upright and stitching done from left to right. The needle is entered from the front. Start at the left and sew about five stitches per inch. As the seam will be opened out later, do not make the stitches excessively tight or it may be impossible to keep the seam flat (Fig. 7*c*). After sewing the length of the seam, open it out and press it flat. Light hammering may be needed.

For a bag-shaped article, the job will have to be made inside-out. If the round seam is used to fix in a round bottom to a kit bag, the edge of the bottom will have to be turned over a little at a time, as stitching progresses. When the seam is completed, the bag must be turned the right way. If the stitches are too tight, there may be difficulty in making the bag take up a good form.

CHAPTER III

SPECIAL STITCHES

A USEFUL stitch, with several applications, is the herringbone (Fig. 8). This can be used for small repairs, or for pulling edges together, as when covering a spar with canvas.

The thread is used double and the ends may be knotted—one of the few occasions where this is done. For most stitching the expert canvas worker prefers to have a free end, which is secured

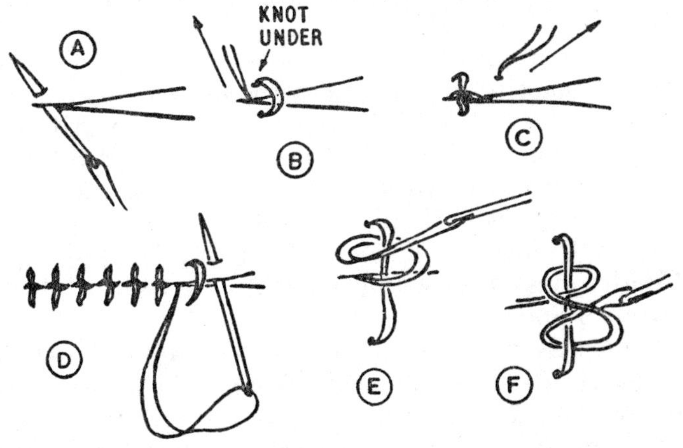

FIG. 8.

by stitching over. Work from the left. Pass the needle up through the far side of the join, so that the knotted end is left underneath (Fig. 8*a*). Pass the needle down through the near side and let the point of the needle come up through the gap, on the left of the thread crossing (Fig. 8*b*). Pull this tight. Hold the tension with the left hand, while the thread is taken over the stitch and the needle entered up through the far side again, to the right of the first stitch (Fig. 8*c*).

As the herringbone stitch usually has to draw the sewn edges together, each stitch should be pulled tight as it is made, and the tension held while the next stitch is made. It is unsatisfactory to try to pull up several stitches together. A finished length of stitching should have the edges even and a neat row of crossing threads along the joint (Fig. 8*d*).

If herringboning is finished by passing the needle back under several stitches before cutting off there is a risk that under tension the stitches may loosen. It is better to make two half hitches around the last stitch. Take a turn around the stitch (Fig. 8*e*), then a second turn so that the two half hitches form a clove hitch (Fig. 8*f*). Finally pass the needle back under two or three stitches and cut off.

There is a variation in the herringbone stitch which is used by some workers. To avoid confusion this is referred to as a sailmaker's stitch (Fig. 9). The effect is very similar, but the needle is entered on both sides from the front, instead of from the back on the far side and the front on the near side. Both times the needle is brought up through the space on the left of the stitch. This gives a greater degree of locking as a stitch is

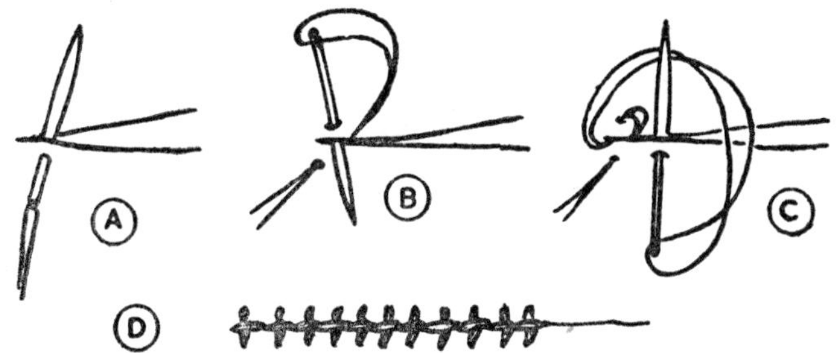

FIG. 9.

made, and may provide a better hold if the edges are tending to pull apart during stitching. The finished seam is thicker, which may be a disadvantage if the joint has to be covered with a patch.

To join two edges with a sailmaker's stitch, start at the left and pass the needle through the near side and up through the space (Fig. 9*a*). Do this again on the far side, bringing the needle up through the space on the left of the crossing thread (Fig. 9*b*). Enter again on the near side and bring the needle up on the left of the crossing thread (Fig. 9*c*). Stitching is continued in this way as far as necessary. As each stitch is made the twist which forms should be adjusted so as to come along the joint (Fig. 9*d*). This is shown loosely, to illustrate the form of the stitches, but of course each stitch should be tightened as it is made.

The thread ends at the start may be laid along the joint and sewn over. If the tension is expected to be too great for this to hold, they may be tied into the first stitch. At the other end, the thread should be fixed to the last stitch with two half hitches and the thread taken under two or three stitches before cutting off.

A simple zig-zag stitch is also described as a herringbone stitch (Fig. 10*a*), but this is not as satisfactory as the two other examples. If the stitch is used, a curved needle is an advantage.

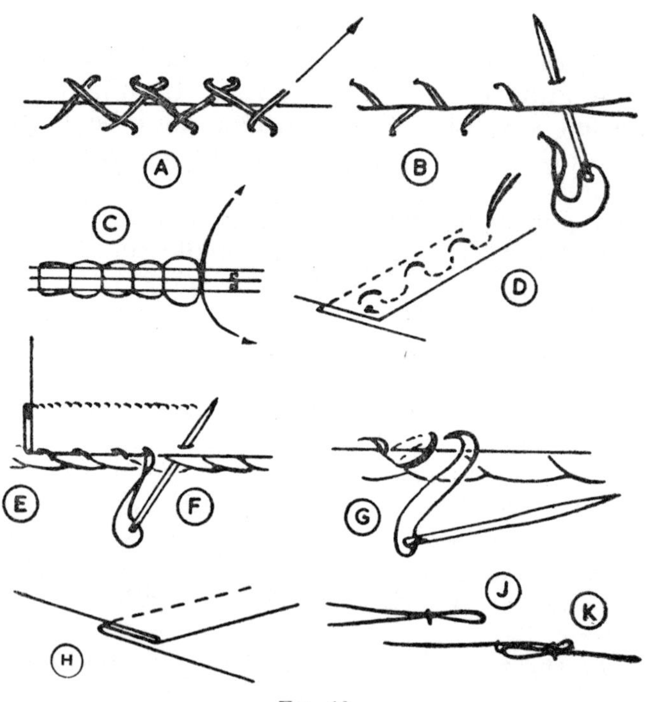

Fig. 10.

Another simple stitch also used for pulling edges together is the baseball stitch (Fig. 10*b*). The thread may be single or double. Both of these stitches are used in leatherwork, but they may have occasional applications in canvaswork. Much sewing of leather is done with two needles. Holes have to be pierced first, then the thread is taken through each hole from opposite sides (Fig. 10*c*). A canvasworker may have to sew leather occasionally, and this shoemaker's stitch will be found to suit most purposes.

One of the simplest stitches is the flat stitch (Fig. 10*d*). The needle is merely taken up and down through the parts being joined. The line of stitching should be straight—a pencil guide line is advisable—and the stitches should all be of the same length. This stitch is not advisable for edge joints. A flat seam is better. The expert rarely uses a flat stitch, except for temporary tacking stitches to hold parts in position while sewing is done, then the tacking stitches are taken out. Of course, tacking stitches can be quite large, but where flat stitching by hand is intended to be permanent the stitches should not be larger than five per inch.

Some canvas parts have to be given roped edges. Roping provides considerable strength. It can be used on the free edges of awnings or covers. At one time all sails had roped edges. Some modern racing sails have their edges arranged in other ways, but cruising and working sails are usually roped, and the only satisfactory way of doing this is by hand.

Canvas to be roped should have a tabled edge, unless the particular construction has already given it a double thickness. This is advisable, even if the edge is a selvedge, as the job is more efficient with a double thickness of canvas. If the tabling is machine-sewn there may be a line of stitches close to the fold. This ensures a straight edge and acts as a guide to the roping stitching, which should be taken over the line of machine stitching.

There are some considerations affecting the fit of canvas and rope, and these are discussed in Chapter six, but the basic stitching is straightforward. With most rope, the thrust needed to get the needle through is greater than in other sewing, so there is an advantage in using the stouter roping palm, although an ordinary palm can be used if that is the only type available.

Have the canvas edge over the rope (Fig. 10*e*). Use double thread and a stout needle. Each stitch has to take up one strand of the rope. To avoid twisting the rope, enter the needle under each strand close to the edge of the canvas, so that all stitches come in the same line along the rope. At the start, lay an inch or so of the ends of the thread along the rope and sew over them. Work from the left, if the rope is the usual right-handed lay. The thickness of the rope strands will determine the size of the stitches (Fig. 10*f*).

Roping may include a splice or it may finish

before the end of the canvas. At these points or anywhere subject to extra strain the last stitch, or several stitches, may be doubled. The thread is taken around the same rope strand, but the needle goes through the canvas a short distance away from the first stitch (Fig. 10*g*). In any case, make sure that the end of the thread is secure and the joint cannot loosen. There is some advantage in dulling the point of a needle used for roping. It is less likely then to catch in the fibres of the strands. The thread should go around the strand each time and not through part of it.

For a sail to keep its shape it has to be made up in comparatively narrow cloths. With cotton or flax, obtained in wide pieces, false seams may be used instead of cutting to narrow widths. At intervals of, say, 12 in. the cloth is gathered into a Z section (Fig. 10*h*), so that it appears similar to the actual seams. A pencil line is drawn in the false seam position and the cloth folded on it. At a distance from the fold equal to the width of the seam there is a line of straight machine stitches (Fig. 10*j*). The cloth is folded back and another line of stitches run down the other side of the false seam (Fig. 10*k*). The finished false seam should be almost impossible to distinguish from the actual seams. In modern sailmaking seams, whether false or actual, would not be done by hand.

CHAPTER IV

ATTACHMENTS

MANY things have to be attached to canvas articles—not many of them are straightforward sewn canvas only. Fasteners, eyelets and many other fittings can be attached without sewing.

An eye of some sort is often needed for attaching a line or fixing the canvas to a hook. For

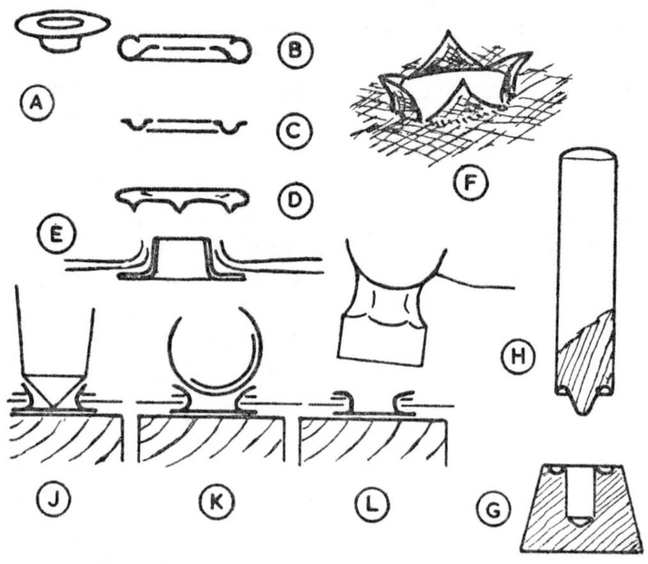

FIG. 11.

most purposes a brass eyelet can be used. The simplest one consists of a ring with a tubular piece standing at the centre, this goes through the canvas and is spread on the other side (Fig. 11*a*). This arrangement is not very secure in canvas, although it is satisfactory in leather. A better eyelet has a ring for the tubular piece to be spread over. A plain ring has an approximately circular cross-section (Fig. 11*b*). If a turnover ring is specified, it has a flat grooved section (Fig. 11*c*). Eyelets with grommet rings have spur teeth below the rings to grip the fabric (Fig. 11*d*).

Eyelets are supplied in gross or one-hundred packets. Those intended for canvas are usually described as 'sail' eyelets. In Britain eyelets are listed by number. A letter B after the number indicates a turnover ring. Without the letter, plain rings are supplied. The usual sizes available are from 3/16 in. internal diameter upwards. Although they are made in sizes at least up to $1\frac{1}{4}$ in. internal diameter (Fig. 12), only those up to $\frac{5}{8}$ in. are commonly used, and for larger holes other arrangements are used.

Although the obvious way to prepare canvas for an eyelet would seem to be to punch a hole of the right size, this is unsatisfactory and weak For small eyelets it is better to make the hole by pushing through a spike in the same direction as the tubular part of the eyelet is to go. By doing this, none of the canvas is removed and the surplus stands up the tube of the eyelet (Fig. 11*e*) to be pinched by it when it is turned over.

If a sufficiently large hole cannot be made in this way, a small hole may be punched and enlarged by pushing through a spike or a fid.

EYELET SIZES

Size	Outside diam. in.	Inside diam. in.	Size	Outside diam. in.	Inside diam. in.
Grommet eyelets			24	$\frac{11}{16}$	$\frac{3}{8}$
000	$\frac{13}{32}$	$\frac{3}{16}$	25	$\frac{3}{4}$	$\frac{13}{32}$
00	$\frac{9}{16}$	$\frac{1}{4}$	26	$\frac{13}{16}$	$\frac{7}{16}$
0	$\frac{11}{16}$	$\frac{3}{8}$	27	$\frac{7}{8}$	$\frac{15}{32}$
1	$\frac{13}{16}$	$\frac{7}{16}$	28	$\frac{15}{16}$	$\frac{1}{2}$
2	$\frac{15}{16}$	$\frac{1}{2}$	29	1	$\frac{9}{16}$
3	1	$\frac{9}{16}$	30	$1\frac{1}{8}$	$\frac{5}{8}$
4	$1\frac{1}{8}$	$\frac{5}{8}$	31	$1\frac{1}{4}$	$\frac{11}{16}$
5	$1\frac{3}{8}$	$\frac{11}{16}$	32	$1\frac{3}{8}$	$\frac{3}{4}$
6	$1\frac{9}{16}$	$\frac{13}{16}$	33	$1\frac{1}{2}$	$\frac{13}{16}$
7	$1\frac{3}{4}$	$\frac{15}{16}$	34	$1\frac{5}{8}$	$\frac{7}{8}$
8	$1\frac{7}{8}$	$1\frac{1}{16}$	35	$1\frac{3}{4}$	1
Ordinary eyelets			36	$1\frac{7}{8}$	$1\frac{1}{8}$
18	$\frac{3}{8}$	$\frac{3}{16}$	37	2	$1\frac{1}{4}$
19	$\frac{7}{16}$	$\frac{7}{32}$			
20	$\frac{15}{32}$	$\frac{1}{4}$			
21	$\frac{1}{2}$	$\frac{9}{32}$			
22	$\frac{9}{16}$	$\frac{5}{16}$			
23	$\frac{5}{8}$	$\frac{11}{32}$			

Note: Sizes upwards of No. 28 are usually only available with turnover rings.

FIG. 12.

An alternative for really large holes is to cut across, so that triangular pieces stand up (Fig. 11*f*).

Punches and dies are available for fixing eyelets, and if much eyeletting is to be done these tools should be obtained. The die consists of a stout iron block shaped to support the main part of the eyelet (Fig. 11*g*). The punch is a convenient size for holding, with an end formed so that it spreads the tube and closes it over the ring (Fig. 11*h*). For the smaller sizes there are plier-type tools which perform the same action, but a separate punch used with a hammer makes a tighter job.

It is possible to fix an occasional small eyelet without special tools. Spreading may be started with a centre punch while the eyelet is supported on a piece of wood (Fig. 11*j*). This is followed by hammering a steel ball (Fig. 11*k*) or the pall pein of an engineer's hammer. Finally, the eyelet is completely closed by direct hammering (Fig. 11*l*).

An alternative to an eyelet is to sew in a metal ring or a rope grommet. For a place where there may be a considerable strain, as where an awning or tent pole has its spike through the canvas, this is preferable to the eyelet, which may be forced out under the strain.

A round-sectioned brass or galvanized iron ring may be used, of a slightly larger inside diameter than the final hole is to be. Two cuts are made across the canvas so that four triangular pieces can stand up inside the ring. If the ring is thin in relation to the size of the hole, these pieces can wrap right over it. If it is thicker, they must be wrapped as far as possible.

With a doubled threads titches are made around

the ring (Fig. 13*a*) as close as possible. They should touch each other in the inside of the hole. Although they will look neater if all the same length, they will be stronger if the lengths vary

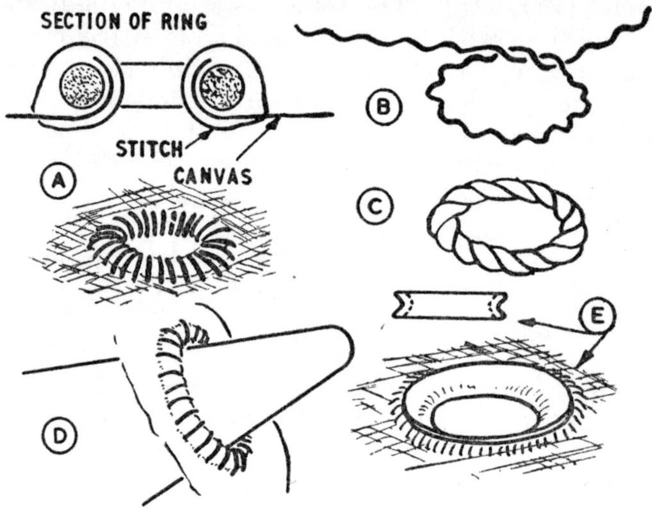

Fig 13.

slightly and care is taken to avoid having adjacent stitches picking up the same threads of the canvas. Start sewing by covering the ends with a few stitches and finish by passing the needle back under three or four stitches.

If a soft eye is wanted, a rope grommet can be sewn in instead of the metal ring. A grommet is made from a single strand of rope about 3½ times as long as the final circumference of the ring is intended to be.

The strand should be taken from ordinary three-stranded rope carefully so that the natural lay is not disturbed. It is formed into a ring and the opposite ends twisted together so that the strand is laid up in the spaces left by the other two strands (Fig. 13*b*). Laying up in this way is continued until three complete circuits are made and the ring has the appearance of a continuous piece of rope (Fig. 13*c*). For sewing into canvas it will be satisfactory to merely cut off the ends, but for a grommet that will not be supported by sewing, the ends should be tapered and tucked into the rope in the same way as when splicing. The grommet is sewn into the canvas in the same way as described for the metal ring.

The stitches inside a grommet or ring which has to fit over a spike or take a metal attachment may chafe. To prevent this it is possible to put a metal thimble inside the hole. It would be possible in some cases to use an ordinary eyelet, but an ordinary machine-made round thimble can be used. These are bell-mouthed on both sides. A soft rope grommet is used first. The size has to be judged so that it will fit into the groove of the thimble after allowing for the canvas and stitches. To get the thimble in, the sewn grommet is expanded by forcing over a fid (Fig. 13*d*), then the thimble put in quickly, before the grommet has gone back to its normal size again (Fig. 13*e*).

If a loop of rope is needed on the side of a piece of canvas, this is known as a cringle.

There may be two eyelets or sewn-in rings or grommets. The cringle is made in a similar way to a grommet. Unlay a single strand without disturbing the lay. Its length should be about $3\frac{1}{2}$ times the final length.

Put the strand through one of the eyelets, keeping one end (X) twice as long as the other (Y) (Fig. 14*a*). Twist the two ends together in the same direction as the original lay for a sufficient length, then pass end X through the second eyelet (Fig. 14*b*). Lay it back around the cringle, filling up the space to make a three-strand rope. Put both ends through the eyelets (Fig. 14*c*). Even up the tension in the cringle before finishing off. Tuck the ends into the cringle in the same way as splicing—tuck an end under a main strand against the lay and over the next strand. For neatness scrape away about half the fibres of the end and tuck again, over and under one. This should be sufficient (Fig. 14*d*).

A variation is to lay in the strands instead of tucking them at each end. Continue until the top of the cringle is reached from each end, making the cringle into a four-strand rope. The meeting ends are tapered, lapped over each other and tucked under adjoining strands.

If the canvas edge is roped, the cringle may be worked into the roping and there is no need for eyelets. The strand for the cringle is at least $3\frac{1}{2}$ times the final length of the cringle. One end is tucked under a strand of the bolt rope on the canvas, leaving enough for splicing tucks later.

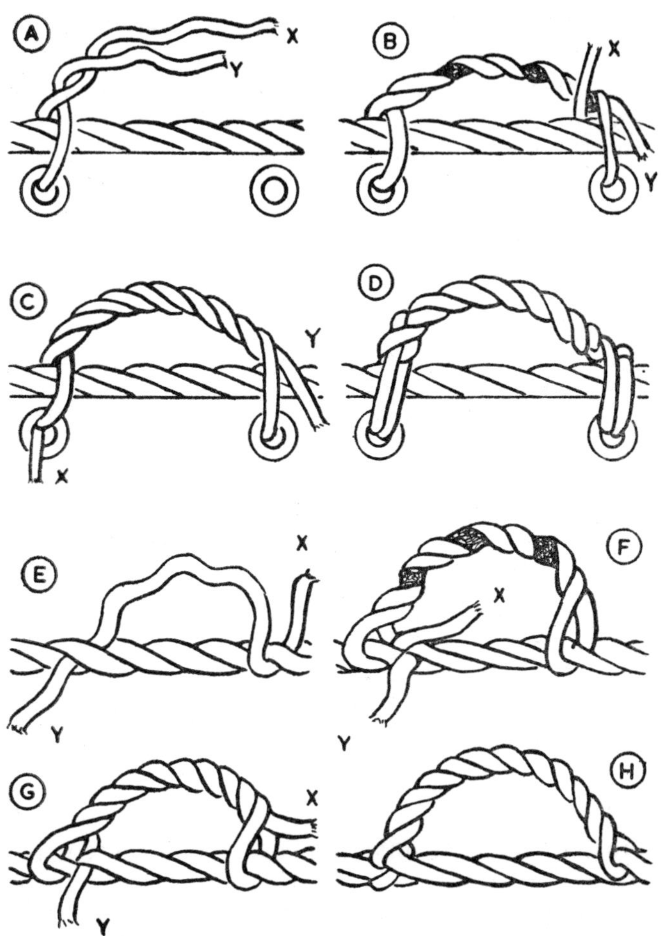

FIG. 14.

The other end is tucked under a strand in a suitable position (Fig. 14*e*). Double the long end back around itself, following the lay, then take it under another bolt rope strand at the first end (Fig. 14*f*). Work back to make the cringle three-stranded (Fig. 14*g*). Tuck the ends into the bolt rope, over and under one, a total of three times each (Fig. 14*h*). For neatness, taper the ends after the first tuck.

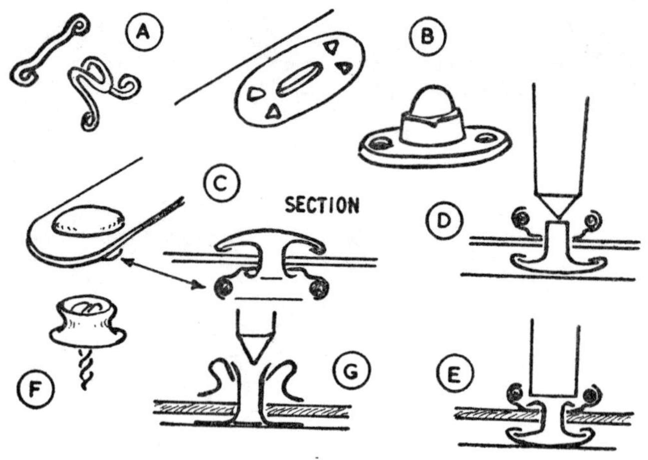

Fig. 15.

Many types of fastener are used on canvas work. The simplest is the hook and eye. These are made of stout wire and are sewn on with plenty of stitches through the eyes (Fig. 15*a*). As with most other things attached to canvas, there should be local reinforcing to take the strain. Stitches should vary in length to spread the strain over different threads in the canvas, but tension should be kept even. The sewing thread should be knotted around stitches at the start and finish.

Small turnbutton fasteners are easy to fix. The upper piece consists of a shaped front with a hole, and lugs projecting from the back. There is a matching piece to take the lugs. A hole may be punched or cut, large enough to clear the turnbutton. If the front piece is placed in position the holes for the lugs can be marked with a pencil. On some canvas a light tap with a hammer will mark where they come. Make holes for the lugs with a spike or the point of a knife. Pad the bench or a piece of wood with a scrap of canvas. Put the front piece in position with the lugs through the holes and rest it face downwards on the padding. Put the matching piece over the lugs and hammer them over lightly (Fig. 15*b*). Heavy hammering may break the lugs or buckle the front.

The lower part, with the turnbutton, may be bought with a base suitable for screwing to wood. If it has to be fixed to canvas it can be fitted in the same way as the top part, with lugs through the canvas to a plate behind.

A 'Lift-the-dot' fastener is a spring fastener. The lower part has a grooved peg projecting. The upper part has a hole and spring. This engages with the grooved peg and will not pull off, but it can be released by lifting the upper part at the point marked with a dot. The method of fitting to canvas is the same as the turnbutton type.

Substantial press studs are available for canvas work. When fitted, the upper part has a domed appearance on the outside. Under this is a hollow with a circular spring. The lower part has a grooved projection, over which the spring will clip. The grip is strong enough to resist a moderate pull, but a strong pull, particularly directly away from the lower part, will release the stud. The lower part may screw to wood or another pattern will fix to canvas.

There are special tools, similar in general construction to the punch and die for fixing eyelets, and these should be obtained if many studs are to be fixed, but small numbers can be fixed with ordinary tools.

For fixing the top part a hole should be made to allow the tubular centre of the domed part to be pushed through. This can be punched undersize and forced out with a spike. The part containing the spring slips over the end of the tube (Fig. 15*c*). With proper fixing tools the domed part rests in a die and a special punch spreads the tubular part inside the inner part. The alternative is to support the domed part on padded wood. A centre punch starts spreading the tube (Fig. 15*d*). This is followed by a flat punch (Fig. 15*e*), which can be any piece of round rod, or even the head end of a large nail.

The tubular centre is long enough to allow for going through several thicknesses of canvas. If the total thickness is rather thin, spreading the normal length of tube may result in it interfering with the action of the spring. It is better to file a small amount off the end of the tube before fixing. If the tube projects through about one-sixteenth inch that is sufficient.

If the lower part is to be fixed to wood, this is done with a screw through the centre (Fig. 15*f*). If the lower part is to fix to canvas, it is in two pieces. The part which connects to the upper part is made with a countersunk hole at the centre. The second piece has a flat back and a tubular projection to fit the countersunk hole. This goes through the canvas. The flat back is put on something solid and the tube spread into the countersink with a centre punch (Fig. 15*g*). The length of the tube in this part is not so critical and the normal length will suit many different thicknesses.

When two canvas sheets have to be overlapped and secured to each other, Dutch lacing makes a good fastening (Fig. 16*a*). This is used for tent doors and for making up long lengths of screening. The rope loops have to be made a suitable length to pass through an eyelet or grommet and hang down just far enough for the loop coming through the next eyelets to engage with them. The closeness of the eyelets depends on the amount of privacy or draughtproofness needed, but 4 in. to 8 in. should suit most purposes. Loops are used for the full depth except for the last position, where there may be a single length of rope for fastening off to a peg or other anchorage.

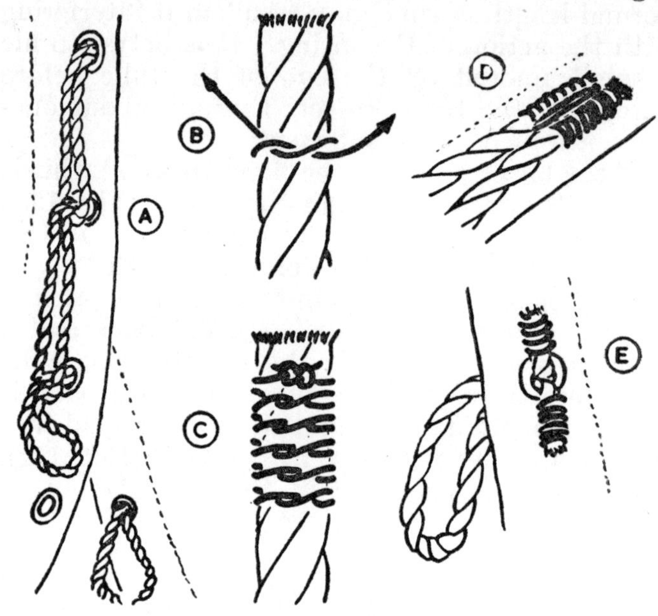

FIG. 16.

When rope has to be sewn to canvas it is always advisable to whip the ends first. Otherwise the strands may untwist and stitches slip off. One of the simplest and most effective whippings is the West Country whipping. Use a length of waxed seaming twine. Put its middle behind the rope and cross the ends in an overhand knot in front (Fig. 16*b*). Take the ends behind and make another overhand knot there. Pull as tight as possible, each time. Continue along the rope, making overhand knots back and front, keeping the turns close together. Do this until the length of the whipping is about the same as the diameter of the rope, then make the last overhand knot into a reef knot (Fig. 16*c*).

For Dutch lacing, the ends of the rope may be put together on the surface of the canvas and sewn over (Fig. 16*d*). Some stitches may go around both ends and some may go through the ropes. A few stitches lengthways between the ropes will tighten the stitches across the rope. An alternative is to take the ends through holes, preferably made with grommets and a tight fit around the doubled rope. At the back the ends are spread and sewn separately (Fig. 16*e*).

CHAPTER V

REPAIRS

MUCH hand sewing which has to be done is connected with repairs. If patches have to be put on or sections replaced, it is advisable to match up the canvas as near as possible, not only in the grade and type, but in the age. If new canvas is used to repair old and stretched material, the new material may eventually stretch and become baggy or pucker. Obviously, the patching material should be sound, but if it has had some use, it may be more satisfactory and less conspicuous than a new piece.

Repairs should be done on the spot to damaged sails and other canvas subject to strain, otherwise the damage may quickly develop into something worse. The repair may only be temporary, although the work which can be done on the spot to minor damage will probably be all that is needed.

The herringbone (Fig. 8) or the sailmakers' stitch (Fig. 9) should be used for small rips. For a small tear stitches should be made as close together as possible (Fig. 17*a*). They can be of varying length. This allows closer stitching and also spreads any strain over different threads of the canvas. Close stitching in this way makes a surprisingly windproof joint, and no other treatment is needed.

The herringbone stitch is not waterproof, of course, and a repair to a canvas canoe or folding boat will also need a patch fixed with adhesive. The adhesive must not be expected to withstand much strain. The load should be taken by stitching and the patch regarded only as the means of keeping water out. For a rip in a canvas canoe, stitches about four or five to the inch should be sufficient to pull the edges together and take any strain.

Any stuck-on patch should be of similar material to that being repaired, although it may be of a lighter grade. It should be given ample overlap and be cut with rounded corners (Fig. 17*b*). Square corners tend to curl back, whatever

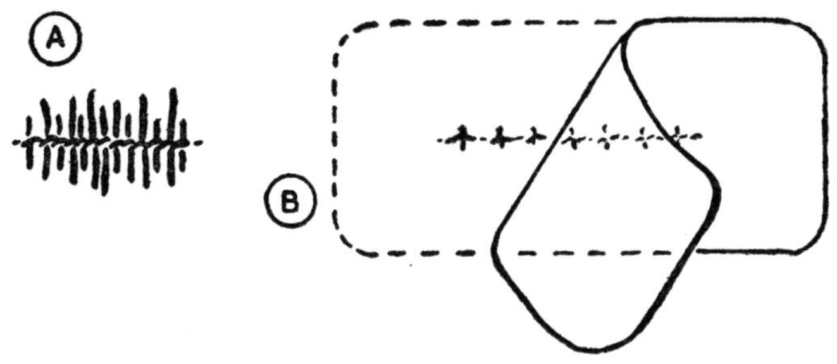

Fig. 17.

adhesive is used.

The part being repaired must be dry. No adhesive will stick to a wet surface and produce a waterproof joint, as the joint then is only the strength of a film of water. On most waters today there is oil on the surface. This, on the canvas, may affect the strength of the adhesive.

Wiping with a cloth soaked in methylated spriits will remove both water and grease. If the canvas has been painted, most of the paint around the damage should be removed by sanding or scraping. In any case the gloss should be removed. Besides cleaning, P.V.C. and rubber coated fabric should be roughened by rubbing with glass-paper.

There are self-adhesive strips of P.V.C. coated material, which are fully waterproof, obtainable in several colours and different thicknesses. Various widths are made. A canoeist should carry a roll of 2 in. or 3 in. width. This can be applied directly over damage and the canoe launched immediately. Normally, a patch on the outside is sufficient, but if the inside is accessible, another patch may be put there. Similar self-adhesive strip is used for repairing nylon spinnaker sails.

Where patches are made from matching material, instead of using self-adhesive strip, a suitable adhesive must be used. Unfortunately there is no waterproof adhesive available which is applicable to all materials. For rubberized materials, ordinary rubber solution, as used for car tyre repairs, may be used. Cut the patching material and roughen both meeting surfaces. Make sure that adhesive covers all the surface, particularly right out to the edges of the patch. Spread it as evenly as possible, but keep it thin. Leave until both surfaces are only just tacky to the touch, then press the patch into position. Use plenty of pressure. If it is a large patch lower it on from one end and press as you go to squeeze out air bubbles. If possible, keep up pressure for a minute or two. If it is a folding canoe or boat, avoid folding over the patch and sprinkle it with french chalk before packing, as surplus adhesive tends to remain slightly sticky for some time.

Ordinary rubber solution is not a reliable adhesive for other materials, although it has some upholstery applications. For canvas made of natural fibres there is the black rubberlike cement, of which Bostik C is a well-known example. It can be used for canvas-to-canvas or canvas-to-wood. If the canvas has been painted or proofed, it should be rubbed with coarse abrasive paper just before joining. Spread the cement on both surfaces and leave until almost dry to the touch, which may take up to 30 minutes. The delay is essential for a good joint. When the surfaces are ready, bring them together without trying to slide them. Press and rub firmly.

For some plastic coating there is no satisfactory adhesive. Some plastics can be welded with heat, but getting the correct heat can only be done satisfactorily in factory conditions. There are some clear adhesives for other plastics. Besides their uses on smooth coatings they may stick to woven synthetic canvas. Follow the directions carefully. Some plastics have a greasiness that interferes with adhesion. They should be wiped with a solvent or be rubbed with an abrasive just before applying the adhesive. If a patch is being applied, cut it to shape with rounded corners, to minimise the risk of peeling, and mark its outline on the surface, so adhesive can be applied without a disfiguring excess on the surrounding surface. Lower the patch on from one side, stroking out air as you progress, otherwise you may find it impossible to remove a bubble of air trapped away from the edge of the patch.

An adhesive with limited uses is the white ammonia-smelling latex adhesive, of which Copydex is a well-known example. This cannot be used on some proofings, but for unproofed natural fibre canvas and almost any open-weave material, this makes a quick and secure repair. Hessian and other coarse open materials can be stuck with it.

Both surfaces are coated fairly liberally, then they are brought together and hammered, so that the adhesive is forced into the weave.

Canvas often tears with an L-shaped rip. A small one may be repaired by herringboning, but a bigger one or more severe damage will have to be patched. Whatever the shape of the damage it is usual to square it up and repair in line with the weft and warp. It may be convenient to trim the damage square before patching, but it may be easier to keep the whole thing in shape if the damage is left until after the patch has been applied. It may even be advisable to pull the torn edges together temporarily to keep the work in shape. After the patch has been fixed, the damage can be trimmed to shape.

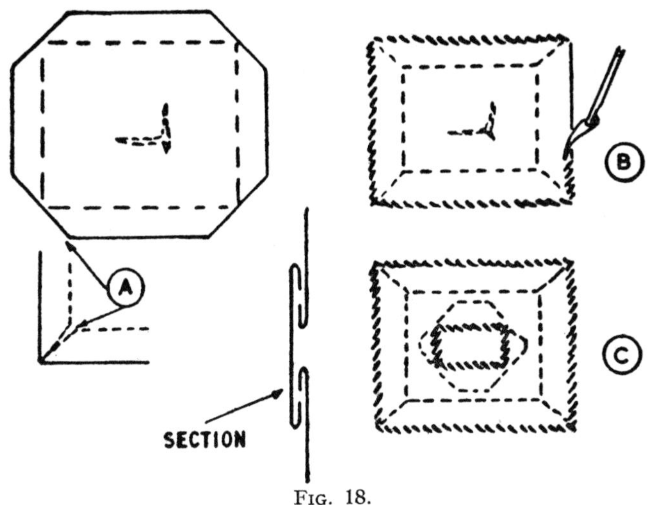

Fig. 18.

The patch is made with a good overlap and is arranged with its edges turned in. If the corners are cut off they will fall into a neat mitre which will lie flat (Fig. 18*a*). Rub down the folds. Either pin the patch in place or lightly tack it with a few stitches near the corners. Sew around the edges (Fig. 18*b*) in the same way as described for tabling (Fig. 5). Keep the job stretched so that puckers are avoided. Move it or yourself around so that each edge is tackled from right to left on the side away from you. When all four edges have been sewn, remove any tacking stitches and turn the work over.

Mark an outline around the damage parallel with the stitches on the edge of the patch. Cut this out and make short cuts at each corner so that the edges may be turned under (Fig. 18*c*). Sew these edges to the patch in the same way as the outer lines of stitching.

More extensive damage may necessitate going back to seams and unpicking their stitches so that new sections of cloth may be put in. A part of a section may be flat-seamed to the remainder of the section and the method of joining to neighbouring parts repeated on the new cloth.

A burn hole or other small round damage may be darned, in the same way as a sock. Doubled seaming twine is used to make parallel threads in one direction, then lines are made to weave across them. This will avoid patching, but darning canvas is only really suitable for small work.

A torn edge or pulled-out eyelet can be repaired with a piece of cloth wrapped over the edge and carried far enough along the edge to spread the strain. The shape of the patch depends on the extent of the damage, but it should go well over the cloth and may have to extend equally on both sides. The edges should be turned in and sewn around, taking in both sides with each stitch if possible.

CHAPTER VI

APPLICATION AND CONSTRUCTION

ONCE the technique of stitching and other canvas working has been mastered, the application of the various processes is mainly commonsense. The various steps in a construction should be thought out. otherwise a point may be reached where a process has to be undertaken in a situation made difficult or impossible by an earlier process. In general, seaming and other work to produce panels of the right size and shape should be done first. This should be followed by the assembly of units, which are then brought together. Such things as roping and the attachment of eyelets or fasteners usually come last, unless some other process interferes with their completion then.

Bags of various sort make good practice jobs for hand sewing. The amount of canvas involved need only be small and the lengths of seams are moderate. Despite the rather slow work of a beginner, results are achieved in a reasonable time.

A small bag for tools or a repair outfit can be made from a flat piece folded over (Fig. 19*a*). After cutting the piece to size, the top edge is tabled (Fig. 19*b*). If there is to be a draw string the ends of the tabling should be turned under (Fig. 19*c*). The edges are joined with a round seam. Rub them down folded towards the same side as the tabling (Fig. 19*d*). The corners could be mitred, although there will be less risk of a hole if the folds are slightly rounded during stitching.

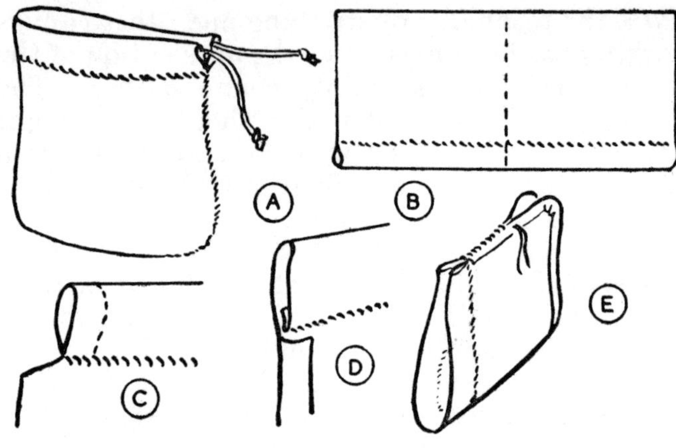

Fig. 19.

Bend over the canvas, with the tabling and folds outwards and commence sewing the round seam below the tabling (Fig. 19*e*). To strengthen this point double the first few stitches. At the corner follow a small curve, letting the folded edges wrinkle. Continue across the bottom and finish off securely close to the fold. Turn the bag the right way. The round seams can be pushed out by pressing down on a post standing endways on the bench. After pushing out, press the seams flat from outside.

The draw string can be threaded through by attaching it to a safety pin, or by using a bodkin.

A bodkin is similar to a needle, but it has a blunt point. A large needle could be adapted by grinding off the point.

A round bag is more roomy. A small bag forms a duffle bag, while a larger one may be used for kit or sails. The geometry of setting out a bag need not be very precise. A simple construction would have a tabled top to take eyelets, a flat seam down the sides and a round seam at the bottom. The length of the canvas would then be enough to allow about ½ in. at the bottom and 1½—2 in. at the top. The circumference of a circle is 3·14 times the diameter. If canvas is cut somewhere between 3¼ and 3½ times the intended diameter, this will be sufficiently accurate for the tubular part of the bag. Of course, sufficient for the seam should also be allowed. The bottom should be the intended diameter plus about 1 in. for the round seam. This can be drawn with a compass or around a suitable plate or metal can. A paper pattern could be used.

Do the tabling first (Fig. 20*a*). Mark and make a flat seam (Fig. 20*b*). Have the bag the right way first, then turn it inside-out for the second row of stitches. At the top the tabled ends may overlap. This involves sewing through several thicknesses, but this is preferable to cutting back the tabling. To sew in the bottom, have the cylinder inside-out and turn down about ½ in. for the seam. The round bottom cannot have its edge rubbed down because of its curve, but a short distance should be turned back just

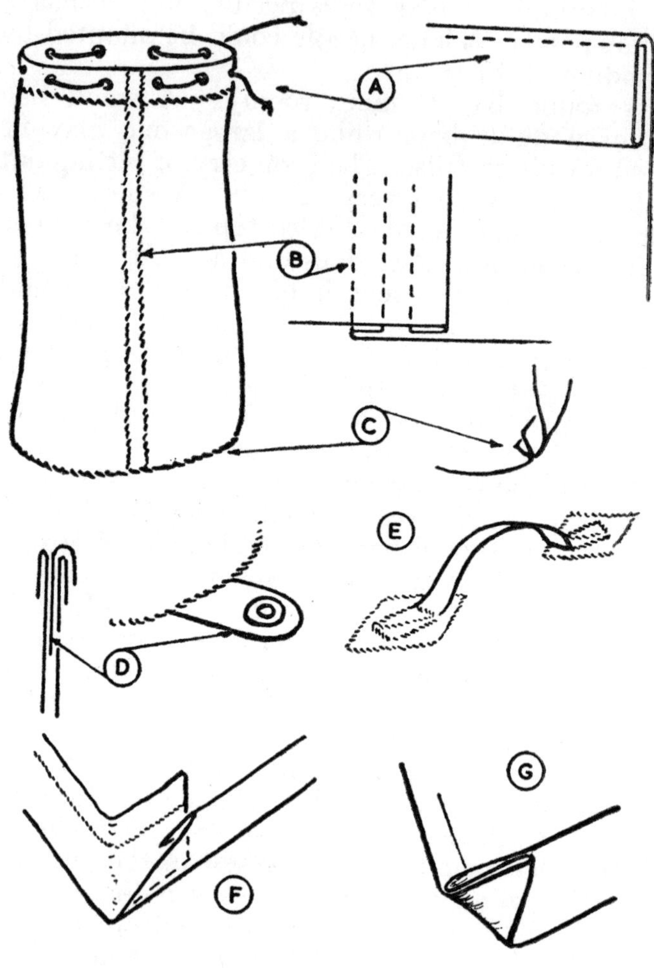

FIG. 20.

ahead of the stitching as the work progresses. Sew around with a round seam in the normal way (Fig. 20*c*) until within a few inches of completion. Check at this point how the cylinder and circle are matching. If there appears to be more of the cylinder than the circle, the amount of the base turned over can be reduced. If the base is too much it can be turned in a little more.

Turn the bag the right way and push the seams into shape. Mark out for the eyelets in the tabling. There should be an even number, otherwise the rope will finish with one end inside and one outside. The eyelets look better if the rings are arranged on the inside.

A duffle bag may have an eyeletted piece at the base to take a rope sling. This can be a piece of webbing, or two pieces of canvas may be round-seamed together and turned inside out. The eyelet is fixed and the piece included in the stitching of the round seam during construction (Fig. 20*d*).

A carrying handle on the side of a bag may be made from a piece of canvas sewn into a tube. The point of attachment should be reinforced. Diamond-shaped patches look neat (Fig. 20*e*). The handle is sewn on in the same way as flat seaming, with doubled stitches near the loop. Flat stitches may be taken across the joint as well. If machine stitches are used, there should be several rows of stitching.

Canvas covers can often be marked in position and this is always preferable to working from measurements. A cover for a boat or trailer, or a cockpit spray cover for a canoe, can be put in position and the outline marked by rubbing a piece of chalk around the outside, so that the line of the edge pressing through is marked. Allowance is then made for the overlap. If a corner has to be boxed, it may be cut and a flap made to overlap (Fig. 20*f*), but a more weatherproof corner will result from folding the fabric (Fig. 20*g*). The triangular piece may be inside or outside, depending on the purpose of the job.

Large constructions may involve right-angled corners. It is important that such things as rick sheets, tents, and awnings should have square corners. This may be marked directly on the canvas, although if the construction involves seaming together many pieces, it is probably better to set out the shape on the floor and fit the canvas over this drawing.

The corners of magazines and sheets of plywood or hardboard are manufactured square. Within their limits these, and other similar things, can be used as set squares for marking out. Larger right angles can be set out geometrically.

Lines up to perhaps 6 ft. can be drawn along a straight piece of wood. Tailor's chalk, which is flat with a thin edge, is useful for marking out canvas. For longer straight lines it is safer to use a chalk line. A piece of seaming twine could be used, but crochet cotton is better. Keep the chalk line on a reel. The free end can have a loop for a spike, or it can be held by an assistant. To use this to draw a line, fix down the end and rub ordinary chalk on it. This is best done by letting the line run off the reel held in one hand while walking backwards from the fixed end and rubbing on chalk with the other hand. When sufficient line has been chalked, stretch the line without jerking it and hold it down with the thumb. If the length is no more than 10 ft. reach towards the centre of the line and lift it a few inches, then release it (Fig. 21*a*). If the length is greater, get an assistant to 'strike' the line.

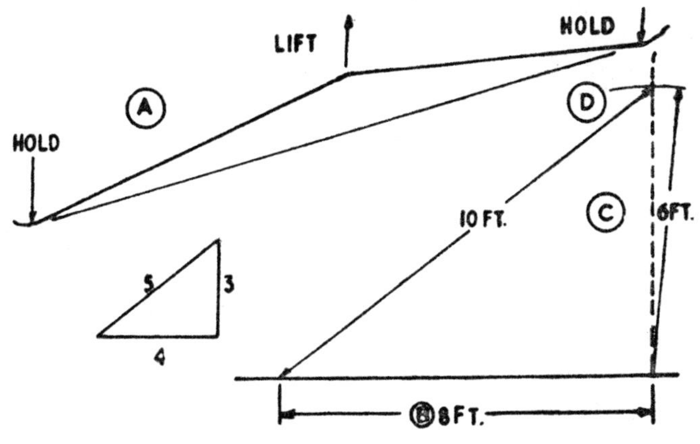

Fig. 21.

To mark out a large right angle the simplest way is to use the fact that if a triangle is drawn with the sides in the proportion 3:4:5, the angle between the two shorter sides will be a right angle. Strike a base line of any convenient length. On this line make two marks at a distance apart equal to four units. The size of the unit depends on the job, but it should result in a triangle bigger than the final job. For an average job the unit might be 2 ft. so the distance along the base line would be 8 ft. (Fig. 21*b*). At the point where the base of the right angle is to be, use a tape measure and a piece of chalk to make an arc of three-unit radius (6 ft. in this case) covering a distance which is estimated to contain the right angle (Fig. 21*c*). From the other point on the base line measure five units to a point on the arc (10 ft. in the example). Mark this point (Fig. 21*d*). A line struck through this point and the basic point on the base line will be at right angles to the base line. If other lines have to be drawn at right angles, they can be measured from this standard right angle.

Roping needs care if the finished job is to keep its shape. Hemp rope is best for ordinary canvas. Terylene may be used with fabric of that material. Some time before work is to commence, the rope should be straightened and stretched with a weight. Before sewing it should appear relaxed. If put down it should remain straight without any inclination to curl or kink. If rope is sewn to canvas without a guide line it may twist and the job will finish with a wavy edge. The relaxed rope should be pulled straight on a flat surface, then a chalk line used to strike a line along it. The chalk deposited would not last for long during sewing, so its course should be marked on the rope at intervals with a pencil or ball pen.

Roping should be done with the canvas stretched moderately in front of the operator who can move along it. For a long roped edge this is better than doing a short length at a time. The line on the rope should be watched so that the rope goes on straight. In use the roping may tend to stretch a little more than the canvas it is sewn to. This can be allowed for by taking up a little more canvas with each stitch. When sewing from left to right, as the needle comes through the rope towards the canvas it should be entered very slightly further to the right than it would naturally go.

If the canvas article is roped all round, the meeting ends should be spliced, preferably with a long splice, which will be inconspicuous. Modern sails are not usually roped all round. Where the roping finishes the neatest effect is obtained by tapering the end of the rope. The alternative is to whip the rope and cut it off. To taper a rope, put a temporary whipping around it some distance from the end (about 9 in. on 1½ in. circumference rope). Unlay the strands. Take each strand in turn and unwind it to expose all of the fibres (Fig. 22*a*). These have to be shaved away progressively from the whipping to the ends. Actually, they may be cut out in a series of steps and this will not be noticeable. If the fibres are well waxed they will stay in place when laid up again. Twist the fibres together in the same way as before.

Take two of the tapered strands and lay them

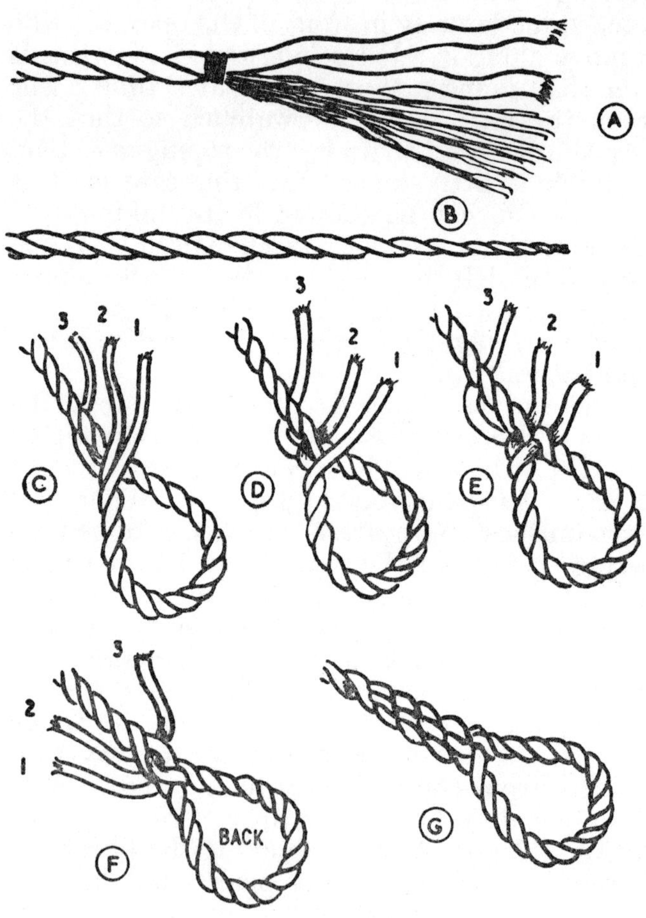

FIG. 22.

up together. As they wrap around each other, give each a slight twist in the direction that will tighten the fibres in the strand. Lay in the third strand in the same way. The final lay should match that of the main body of the rope (Fig. 22*b*). Cut off the whipping.

An eye in the side of a rope can be made by forming a cringle. If the eye is needed in the end of the roping itself it should be spliced. An ordinary eye splice, tucked over-and-under, does not have a good edge for sewing. It is better to use a sailmaker's eye splice. The splice follows the lay of the rope and sewing may be continued in the same way right up the splice and the side of the eye if necessary.

In an ordinary splice the ends are tucked against the lay. In a sailmaker's eye splice the ends are tucked with the lay. Unlay the strands for a short distance and bend up the eye (Fig. 22*c*). Have two strands in front and one behind. Tuck the centre end (No. 2) under a main strand (Fig. 22*d*). Tuck the end nearer the eye under a main strand, going in where the other comes out (Fig. 22*e*). Turn the rope over and tuck the remaining end strand under the only main strand without an end under it, going in with the lay (Fig. 22*f*). This should leave an end projecting from each space. From this point take each end in turn back around the main strand it is already under. Do this for a total of four times. For the neatest finish the strands should be tapered after the first tucks (Fig. 22*g*).

Points of strain should be reinforced. Eyelets, press studs and other fasteners should not be fixed to just a single thickness. The double thickness of a tabled edge may provide sufficient strength. The thickness may be trebled if the inside part of the tabling is full width (Fig. 20*a*). In some cases an extra piece has to be sewn on. This happens at the corners of sails, the attachment points of covers and the fastenings for tent guy lines.

In a corner there may be a triangular piece sewn in (Fig. 23*a*). This goes inside the tabling.

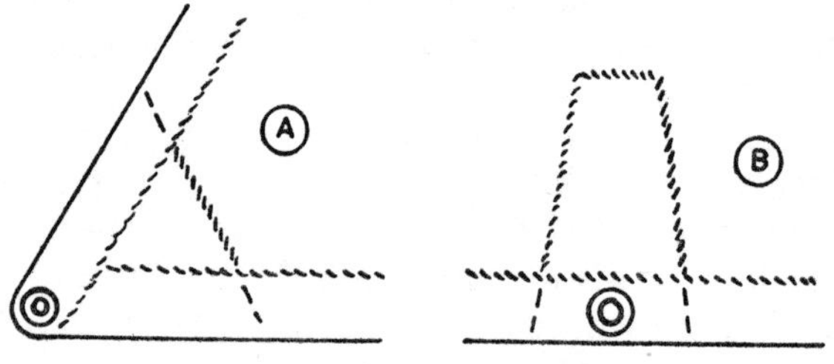

Fig. 23.

Any eyelet or other attachment should go through it. The edge between the tabling is turned under and sewn in the same way as a patch. If the reinforcement is on an edge, it looks better if cut wedge-shaped instead of square (Fig. 23*b*). On some sails or canvas structures of special shape, the reinforcements may be of involved shapes so as to spread the strain evenly.

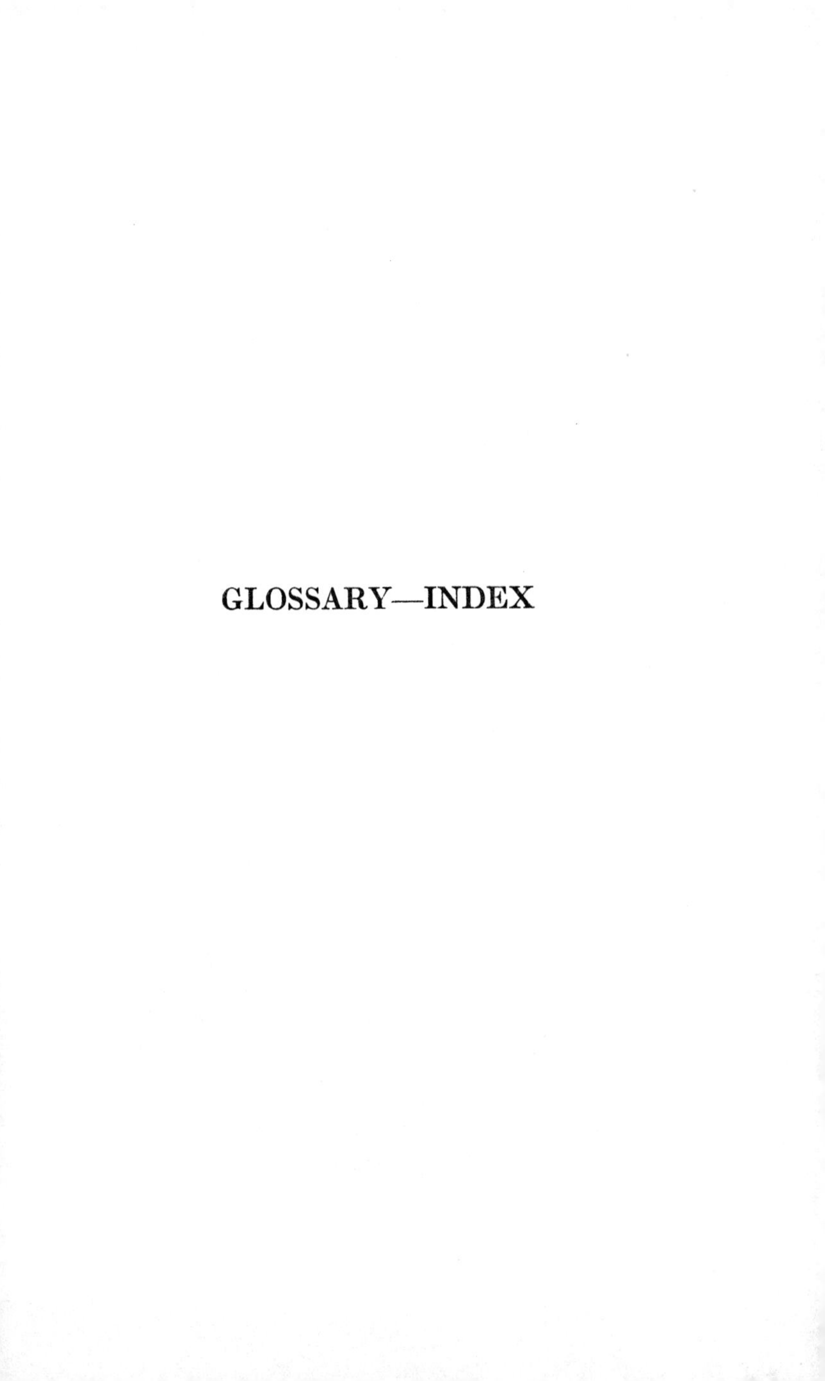

GLOSSARY—INDEX

GLOSSARY-INDEX